Date: 3/7/16

J 796.323 DON
Donnelly, Patrick,
The best NBA forwards of all
time /

THE BEST NBA
FORWARDS
OF ALL TIME

By Patrick Donnelly

www.abdopublishing.com

Published by Abdo Publishing, a division of ABDO, PO Box 398166, Minneapolis, Minnesota 55439. Copyright © 2015 by Abdo Consulting Group, Inc. International copyrights reserved in all countries. No part of this book may be reproduced in any form without written permission from the publisher. SportsZone™ is a trademark and logo of Abdo Publishing.

Printed in the United States of America, North Mankato, Minnesota
032014
092014

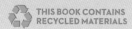
THIS BOOK CONTAINS
RECYCLED MATERIALS

Cover Photos: Charles Krupal/AP Images (left);
Frank Franklin II/ AP Images (right)
Interior Photos: Charles Krupa/AP Images, 1 (left); Frank Franklin II/
AP Images, 1 (right); AP Images, 7, 9, 13, 15, 17, 25, 35, 37; Harold
Matosian/AP Images, 11; John Lent/AP Images, 19; Robert W. Klein/AP
Images, 21; Ray Stubblebine/AP Images, 23; Clem Murray/AP Images,
27; Harry Harris/AP Images, 29; Doug Pizac/AP Images, 31, 45; F. Carter
Smith/AP Images, 33; Bill Janscha/AP Images, 39; David Zalubowski/
AP Images, 41; Rich Pedroncelli/AP Images, 43; Ralk-Fin Hestoft/
AP Images, 47; Jim Mone/AP Images, 49; Tom Strattman/AP Images,
51; Winslow Townson/AP Images, 53; Eric Gay/AP Images, 55, 57, 59;
Michael Conroy/AP Images, 61

Editor: Chrös McDougall
Series Designer: Christa Schneider

Library of Congress Control Number: 2014932920

Cataloging-in-Publication Data
Donnelly, Patrick.
 The best NBA forwards of all time / Patrick Donnelly.
  p. cm. -- (NBA's best ever)
ISBN 978-1-62403-411-4
1. National Basketball Association--Juvenile literature.   2. Forwards
(Basketball)--Juvenile literature.   I. Title.
796.323--dc23

                                        2014932920

TABLE OF CONTENTS

INTRODUCTION

Great forwards have come in all shapes and sizes.

Some of the National Basketball Association's (NBA's) greatest forwards were long and lean. They were graceful athletes who dazzled crowds with their on-court artistry. Others were rugged, powerful players. They dominated the game underneath the basket. And others still were gritty, undersized underdogs. They became superstars through hard work and constant effort. These forwards might have taken different paths to success, but all of them were champions in their own way.

Here are some of the best forwards in NBA history.

BOB PETTIT

Bob Pettit did not want history to repeat in 1958. The previous year, his St. Louis Hawks had faced the Boston Celtics in the NBA Finals. The hard-fought series went to a seventh and deciding game. The Celtics held a late 125–123 lead in double overtime. Pettit had the ball for the last shot. But his game-tying attempt fell off the rim, giving Boston the title.

The teams met again in the 1958 NBA Finals. St. Louis won three of the first five games. The Hawks needed just one more win to take home the crown. Pettit was not going to let Boston force Game 7. So he scored an amazing 50 points in Game 6. That lifted the Hawks to a 110–109 win. They were the NBA champions. It was the team's first title. The Hawks later moved to Atlanta. Through 2013, they still had not won another championship.

The St. Louis Hawks' Bob Pettit (9) battles for the ball with a Philadelphia Warriors player during a 1956 game.

Pettit came out of Louisiana State University as a power forward.

People were not sure he would be successful against bigger, stronger opponents. But Pettit became one of the best players in NBA history. He averaged at least 20 points and 12 rebounds in each of his 11 pro seasons. He also played in 11 All-Star Games. When he retired, Pettit had scored the most points of any player in NBA history. And only one other player had grabbed more rebounds at the time.

Longtime rival Bill Russell praised Pettit for his persistence. "Bob made 'second effort' a part of the sport's vocabulary," Russell said. "He kept coming at you more than any man in the game."

4

The number of All-Star Game Most Valuable Player (MVP) Awards Bob Pettit won in his career. Only Kobe Bryant had matched that through 2013.

St. Louis Hawks forward Bob Pettit leans in for a basket during a 1957 game against the Cincinnati Royals.

BOB PETTIT

Hometown: Baton Rouge, Louisiana

College: Louisiana State University

Height, Weight: 6 feet 9, 205 pounds

Birth Date: December 12, 1932

Team: Milwaukee/St. Louis Hawks (1954–65)

All-Star Games: 11 (1955–65)

MVP Awards: 1955–56, 1958–59

First-Team All-NBA: 1954–55, 1955–56, 1956–57, 1957–58, 1958–59, 1959–60, 1960–61, 1961–62, 1962–63, 1963–64

ELGIN BAYLOR

The Los Angeles Lakers are one of the most famous teams in all of sports.
Many of the greatest players in NBA history made their names while leading the Lakers to NBA titles. It is fair to say, however, that the Lakers' successes might not have been possible without Elgin Baylor.

The Lakers were originally based in Minneapolis. They had great success there. But the team was struggling by the late 1950s. They were not winning games. They were not drawing fans, either. Team owner Bob Short knew he was close to going out of business.

Los Angeles Lakers forward Elgin Baylor powers his way in for a shot against the Philadelphia 76ers in 1964.

But then Short got the first pick in the 1958 NBA Draft. He selected Baylor. And the young player quickly changed the team's fortunes. Baylor was the NBA Rookie of the Year in 1958–59. He also led the Lakers to the NBA Finals that year. He helped guide the Lakers to the playoffs the next year, too.

Those two seasons helped the Lakers stay alive in the NBA. Instead of folding, they moved to Los Angeles in 1960. It was there that they became one of the NBA's most iconic teams.

Baylor put up amazing numbers in Los Angeles. He was the first player to finish a season in the top five in scoring, rebounding, assists, and free-throw percentage. He once scored 71 points in a game. That was the most ever at the time. He also played with a style and flair that was unusual for his day. Many of the great players that followed him patterned their game after Baylor's.

40.03

The average minutes per game Elgin Baylor played throughout his career. That ranked him number five all time through 2013.

The Lakers' Elgin Baylor breaks toward the basket during a 1965 game against the San Francisco Warriors.

ELGIN BAYLOR

Hometown: Washington DC

College: Seattle University

Height, Weight: 6 feet 5, 225 pounds

Birth Date: September 16, 1934

Team: Minneapolis/Los Angeles Lakers (1958–71)

All-Star Games: 11 (1959–65, 1967–70)

First-Team All-NBA: 1958–59, 1959–60, 1960–61, 1961–62, 1962–63, 1963–64, 1964–65, 1966–67, 1967–68, 1968–69

JOHN HAVLICEK

John Havlicek knew someone had to make a play. He decided it might as well be him.

It was Game 7 of the 1965 Eastern Conference finals. His Boston Celtics had a one-point lead in the final seconds of the game. But the Philadelphia 76ers had the ball under Boston's basket. The 76ers needed just one basket to advance to the NBA Finals. If they advanced, they would snap the Celtics' streak of six straight NBA championships.

That is when Havlicek made his move. He jumped in front of the in-bounds pass and tipped it away to teammate Sam Jones. Jones dribbled out the clock to seal the game. Celtics radio announcer Johnny Most was calling the game. His call of that play became one of the most famous lines in sports broadcasting history.

Boston Celtics forward John Havlicek dribbles around a New York Knicks defender during a 1972 playoff game.

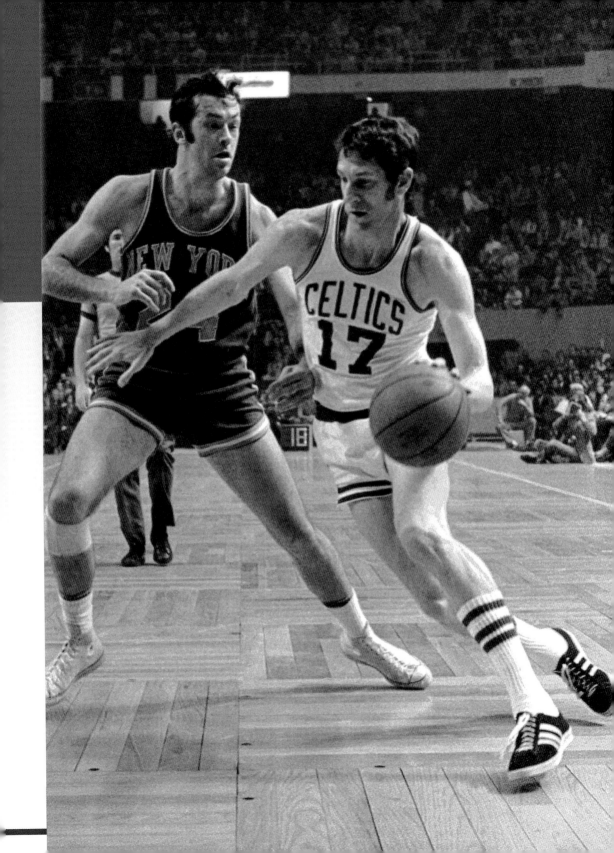

"Havlicek stole the ball!" he shouted. "It's all over! It's all over! Johnny Havlicek is being mobbed by the fans!"

Havlicek was famous for making clutch plays when his team needed them most. He joined the Celtics in 1962. The Celtics had a veteran, championship team that year. So Havlicek did not break into the starting lineup. He often was on the court at the end of the game, though.

For that, Havlicek became the NBA's first well-known sixth man. He came off the bench to give a starter a break. The Celtics did not miss a beat with him on the floor. He was so strong that guards had a hard time defending him. Yet he was quick enough to give forwards trouble, too. Havlicek won six titles as a backup. Then he captained a young Celtics team to two more championships before he retired.

8

The number of NBA titles John Havlicek won. That was third only to teammates Bill Russell and Sam Jones through 2013.

The Celtics' John Havlicek drives to the basket against the Los Angeles Lakers during the 1968 NBA Finals.

JOHN HAVLICEK

Hometown: Martins Ferry, Ohio

College: Ohio State University

Height, Weight: 6 feet 5, 203 pounds

Birth Date: April 8, 1940

Team: Boston Celtics (1962–78)

All-Star Games: 13 (1966–78)

First-Team All-NBA: 1970–71, 1971–72, 1972–73, 1973–74

All-Defensive Team: 1971–72, 1972–73, 1973–74, 1974–75, 1975–76

RICK BARRY

In many ways, Rick Barry was one of a kind. He was a flashy scorer. He was one of the best passers of his day. But he also had a hot temper. He had constant clashes with coaches, owners, teammates, and opponents. He also was one of the first NBA stars to leave for the rival American Basketball Association (ABA). The ABA challenged the NBA during the 1960s and 1970s.

More than anywhere else, though, Barry stood out at the free-throw line. Most players used the modern overhand shot for free throws by the 1960s. But Barry shot his underhand. He did not care if other people thought he looked silly. He did not care that the "granny shot" went out of style in the 1950s. All he cared about was putting the ball through the hoop.

Forward Rick Barry of the New York Nets goes up for a basket against the Kentucky Colonels during a 1971 ABA game.

And Barry did that better than any forward in basketball history. He made 90 percent of his NBA free throws. That was third best in NBA history through 2013. He led his league in free-throw percentage seven times. His willingness to "look silly" led to a lot of points for his teams.

118

The number of points Rick Barry scored in the 1975 NBA Finals. That record for a four-game series stood until 1995.

Barry was an All-Star in his first two seasons with the San Francisco Warriors. He led the NBA with 35.6 points per game his second year. Then he jumped to the ABA. Barry had to sit out a full season due to a legal dispute over his contract. He eventually played four seasons in the ABA. His career ended back in the NBA, though. And in 1975, Barry led the Warriors to their only NBA title in the Bay Area through 2013.

The San Francisco Warriors' Rick Barry moves the ball down the court against the Cincinnati Royals during a 1966 game.

RICK BARRY

Hometown: Elizabeth, New Jersey

College: University of Miami

Height, Weight: 6 feet 7, 205 pounds

Birth Date: March 28, 1944

Teams: San Francisco Warriors (1965–67)*
  Oakland Oaks (1968–69)
  Washington Capitols (1969–70)
  New York Nets (1970–72)
  Golden State Warriors (1972–78)
  Houston Rockets (1978–80)

All-Star Games: 12 (1966–67, 1969–78)*

First-Team All-NBA: 1965–66, 1966–67, 1968–69, 1969–70, 1970–71, 1971–72, 1973–74, 1974–75, 1975–76*

* Stats from 1968 to 1972 are from ABA

ELVIN HAYES

On the biggest night in college basketball history, Elvin Hayes was the game's biggest star. It was 1968. The top-ranked University of California, Los Angeles Bruins had won 47 straight games. But Hayes and his second-ranked University of Houston Cougars beat them 71–69. It became known as the "Game of the Century." And in it, Hayes had 39 points and 15 rebounds.

The man nicknamed "The Big E" was not yet done, though. Hayes was the first pick in the 1968 NBA Draft. He began as a center for the San Diego Rockets. Individually, he was a star. As a rookie, Hayes led the NBA in field goals and points. In his second year, he led the league in rebounds.

The Washington Bullets' Elvin Hayes outreaches New York Knicks defenders for a tip-in in 1978.

Hayes stayed at center when the team moved to Houston in 1971. But the Rockets could not find a winning formula. So in 1972, they traded Hayes to the Baltimore Bullets.

With the Bullets, Hayes moved to power forward. He never matched the high scoring of his early seasons. But he did not need to. Hayes teamed with center Wes Unseld with the Bullets. They formed a fearsome front line. Together, they led the Bullets to the 1978 NBA title. Hayes was a strong defender. He continued to rack up the rebounds. But it was his trademark turn-around jump shot that set him apart.

Hayes also was known for his durability. Through 2013, only three men in NBA history had played more minutes. Hayes still ranked in the top 10 in points and rebounds, as well.

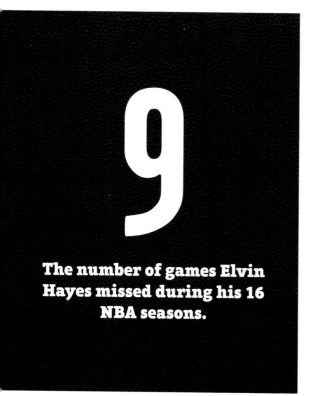

9

The number of games Elvin Hayes missed during his 16 NBA seasons.

Elvin Hayes holds the championship trophy after his Washington Bullets claimed the 1978 NBA title.

ELVIN HAYES

Hometown: Rayville, Louisiana

College: University of Houston

Height, Weight: 6 feet 9, 235 pounds

Birth Date: November 17, 1945

Teams: San Diego/Houston Rockets (1968–72, 1981–84)
Baltimore/Capital/Washington Bullets (1972–81)

All-Star Games: 12 (1969–80)

First-Team All-NBA: 1974–75, 1976–77, 1978–79

JULIUS ERVING

Julius Erving already was a star in the ABA. Then in 1976, he became a national sensation with one famous dunk.

The ABA tried to differentiate itself from the NBA. So in 1976, the league staged the first All-Star Slam Dunk Contest. Erving, also known as "Dr. J," squared off against some of the high-flying greats of the game. But Artis Gilmore, George Gervin, and David Thompson did not stand a chance.

Erving wowed the crowd with a dunk never before seen. He took off on a dead run from center court. Then he leaped from the free-throw line. Flying 15 feet (4.57 m) to the basket, Erving finally slammed the ball through the hoop. That was it. Dr. J was the greatest dunker on the planet.

The Philadelphia 76ers' Julius Erving floats for a layup during a 1981 playoff game against the Boston Celtics.

Erving's game was much more than dunking, however. He was a flashy player. And he was famous for twisting through the air. He could adjust gracefully in mid-flight to avoid defenders. But Erving also was a feared defender. He could block shots, make steals, and grab a lot of rebounds. That helped him win four MVP Awards. One of those came after the ABA and NBA merged in 1976–77.

Erving helped the New York Nets win two ABA titles. He then joined the NBA's Philadelphia 76ers. There, he had a harder time winning the big one. His 76ers fell three times in the NBA Finals. Finally, in 1983, he teamed with Moses Malone to lead the 76ers to the NBA title. Erving retired in 1987. He went down as one of the most popular and exciting players in pro basketball history.

28.7

Julius Erving's per-game scoring average in five ABA seasons. That was second only to Rick Barry.

Julius "Dr. J." Erving scores for the New York Nets during a 1975 ABA game against the Virginia Squires.

JULIUS ERVING

Hometown: Roosevelt, New York

College: University of Massachusetts

Height, Weight: 6 feet 6, 200 pounds

Birth Date: February 22, 1950

Teams: Virginia Squires (1971–73)*
New York Nets (1973–76)
Philadelphia 76ers (1976–87)

All-Star Games: 16 (1972–87)*

MVP Awards: 1973–74, 1974–75, 1975–76, 1980–81*

First-Team All-NBA: 1972–73, 1973–74, 1974–75, 1975–76, 1977–78, 1979–80, 1980–81, 1981–82, 1982–83*

All-Defensive Team: 1975–76*

* Stats from 1976 and earlier are from ABA

29

LARRY
BIRD

Larry Bird's career had started to decline. But one Sunday afternoon in 1988, he showed he still had plenty left in his bag of tricks.

It was Game 7 of the Eastern Conference semifinals. Bird's Boston Celtics squared off against the Atlanta Hawks. And the ancient Boston Garden was rocking. The Hawks' Dominique Wilkins was one of the brightest stars in the league. He made 19 of 33 shots that afternoon. And he finished with 47 points.

Bird entered the fourth quarter with only 14 points. But he would not be denied. He quickly scored nine straight to give Boston the lead. Wilkins then tied the game with around six minutes to play. But Bird again took over.

Boston Celtics forward Larry Bird goes up for a shot against the Los Angles Lakers during the 1984 NBA Finals.

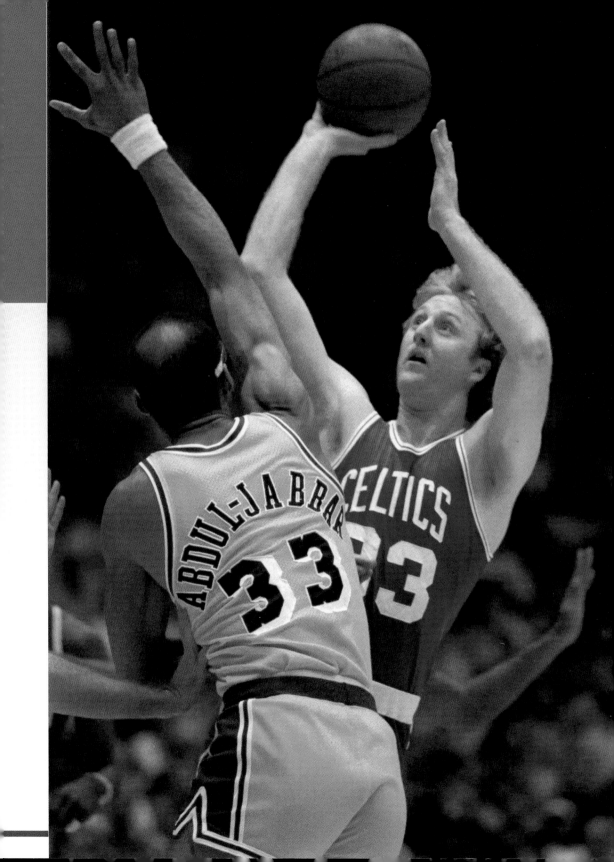

"Larry Legend" scored 11 points in the final six minutes. Among the baskets was a three-pointer with Wilkins's hand in his face. Bird's 20 fourth-quarter points helped his Celtics win a shootout in one of his most memorable games.

Bird was one of the greatest all-around players the NBA has ever seen. He was a brilliant passer and a fine defensive player. His court vision was one of a kind. But Bird made his name as a lights-out shooter. His shooting in 1986–87 was incredible. He shot better than 50 percent from the field and 90 percent from the free-throw line. No player in NBA history had ever done that. Then Bird did it again the next year.

Bird was a member of the original "Dream Team" at the 1992 Olympic Games. He later became a successful coach and general manager of the Indiana Pacers.

3

The number of consecutive NBA MVP Awards Larry Bird won. Only Bill Russell and Wilt Chamberlain had accomplished that feat before Bird.

The Celtics' Larry Bird (33) gives a high five following a win over the Houston Rockets in the 1986 NBA Finals.

LARRY BIRD

Hometown: French Lick, Indiana

College: Indiana State University

Height, Weight: 6 feet 9, 220 pounds

Birth Date: December 7, 1956

Team: Boston Celtics (1979–92)

All-Star Games: 12 (1980–88, 1990–92)

MVP Awards: 1983–84, 1984–85, 1985–86

First-Team All-NBA: 1979–80, 1980–81, 1981–82, 1982–83, 1983–84, 1984–85, 1985–86, 1986–87, 1987–88

KEVIN McHALE

If not for a well-timed growth spurt, Kevin McHale might never have found his way into the NBA, let alone the Hall of Fame. McHale grew up in Hibbing, Minnesota. Hockey was king in the small northern Minnesota town. So McHale naturally saw his future on the ice.

But a funny thing happened on his way to the National Hockey League. McHale began high school at 5 feet 9 inches tall. And he grew more than 12 inches before graduating. So McHale changed his winter sport from hockey to basketball and led Hibbing High School to the state finals.

McHale went on to have a standout basketball career at the University of Minnesota. Many NBA teams were interested in choosing him in the 1980 NBA Draft. The Boston Celtics succeeded.

Boston Celtics forward Kevin McHale dunks against the Houston Rockets during the 1986 NBA Finals.

The Celtics had to swing a trade with the Golden State Warriors to make it happen, though. In the trade, Boston received center Robert Parish and the number three pick. They used that choice to grab McHale. McHale and Parish teamed with Larry Bird to make the Celtics one of the greatest teams of the 1980s.

McHale had unusually long arms and legs. That made him a tough rebounder under the basket. He became known as one of the best offensive forwards in the league. McHale perfected a variety of low-post moves over the years. He used moves such as drop steps, head and ball fakes, up-and-under moves, and turn-around jumpers to get open for shots.

McHale won three NBA titles with the Celtics. He later coached the Minnesota Timberwolves and the Houston Rockets.

.604/.836

Kevin McHale's field goal and free throw percentages in 1986–87. It marked the first time a player had topped .600 and .800 in those stats in the same season.

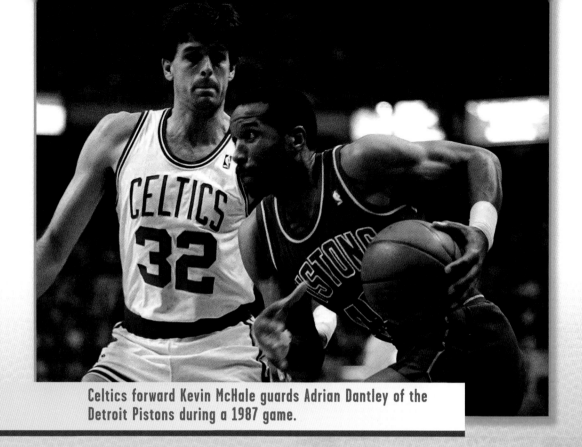

Celtics forward Kevin McHale guards Adrian Dantley of the Detroit Pistons during a 1987 game.

KEVIN McHALE

Hometown: Hibbing, Minnesota

College: University of Minnesota

Height, Weight: 6 feet 10, 210 pounds

Birth Date: December 19, 1957

Team: Boston Celtics (1980–93)

All-Star Games: 7 (1984, 1986–91)

First-Team All-NBA: 1986–87

All-Defensive Team: 1985–86, 1986–87, 1987–88

CHARLES BARKLEY

Charles Barkley almost ate his way out of the NBA before playing his first game. The Philadelphia 76ers drafted Barkley in 1984. He was a dynamic player at Auburn University. But the man nicknamed "The Round Mound of Rebound" was overweight.

Barkley had been the number five pick in the 1984 NBA Draft. Yet he did not get invited to try out for the US Olympic Team that year. He showed up at his first NBA training camp weighing 300 pounds. The 76ers told him he had to get serious about his conditioning.

That is all it took. By the time his rookie season began, Barkley was down to 250 pounds. Before long, he was one of the best forwards in the game.

Charles Barkley of the Phoenix Suns goes up for a shot during a 1995 game against the Dallas Mavericks.

"There is nobody who does what Barkley does," former NBA great Bill Walton said. "He's a dominant rebounder, a dominant defensive player, a three-point shooter, a dribbler, a playmaker."

"Sir Charles," as he also was known, had an outsized personality to match his game. He became a fan and media favorite for his constant chattering. But he had the skills to back up his talk. When he retired, Barkley was one of only four players in NBA history with at least 20,000 points, 10,000 rebounds, and 4,000 assists. The only thing he was missing was an NBA championship.

Barkley did get a second chance at the Olympics, though. And as a member of the 1992 Dream Team, he indeed won a gold medal in Barcelona, Spain. He later became a popular sports broadcaster.

14.6

Charles Barkley's rebounds per game average in 1986–87. He became the shortest player since Harry Gallatin in 1953–54 to win the NBA rebounding title.

Houston Rockets forward Charles Barkley looks to pass during a 1999 game against the Denver Nuggets.

CHARLES BARKLEY

Hometown: Leeds, Alabama

College: Auburn University

Height, Weight: 6 feet 6, 252 pounds

Birth Date: February 20, 1963

Teams: Philadelphia 76ers (1984–92)
Phoenix Suns (1992–96)
Houston Rockets (1996–2000)

All-Star Games: 11 (1987–97)

MVP Award: 1992–93

First-Team All-NBA: 1987–88, 1988–89, 1989–90, 1990–91, 1992–93

KARL MALONE

The Utah Jazz needed a win on the road to stay alive in the 1998 NBA Finals. As usual, "The Mailman" Karl Malone delivered.

The Jazz trailed the Chicago Bulls 3–1 in the series. Utah had lost to the Bulls in six games in the 1997 NBA Finals. Now the Jazz were one game away from losing to the Bulls in five games in 1988.

That is when Malone came through with one of the greatest performances ever in the NBA Finals. He made 17 of 27 shots. Many of those shots came against Chicago's ace defender, Dennis Rodman. Malone also grabbed nine rebounds and dished out five assists. And he hit a late jump shot to seal the 83–81 victory.

Karl Malone of the Utah Jazz goes up for a dunk against the Sacramento Kings during a 1997 game.

The Bulls eventually did win the series. But Malone's heroics were typical of his career with the Jazz. For 18 seasons, he and point guard John Stockton formed the backbone of a strong Utah lineup. Stockton still held the NBA career assists record through 2013. Malone was on the receiving end of many of those assists in Utah's pick-and-roll offense.

1,412

The number of games Karl Malone and John Stockton played together. That was the most of any two teammates in NBA history through 2013.

The Mailman was one of the most physical and durable players of his day. He kept his body in tremendous shape. That helped him withstand the rough action under the hoop. Malone's fitness also allowed him to run the court on the fast break and finish with thundering dunks.

Malone went to the free-throw line more than any player in NBA history. He also made more free throws than any other player. Through 2013, he was number two on the career list for points and minutes played.

Jazz forward Karl Malone goes for a rebound during a 1996 game against the Seattle SuperSonics.

KARL MALONE

Hometown: Summerfield, Louisiana

College: Louisiana Tech University

Height, Weight: 6 feet 9, 250 pounds

Birth Date: July 24, 1963

Teams: Utah Jazz (1985–2003)
Los Angeles Lakers (2003–04)

All-Star Games: 14 (1988–98, 2000–02)

MVP Awards: 1996–97, 1998–99

First-Team All-NBA: 1988–89, 1989–90, 1990–91, 1991–92, 1992–93, 1993–94, 1994–95, 1995–96, 1996–97, 1997–98, 1998–99

All-Defensive Team: 1996–97, 1997–98, 1998–99

SCOTTIE PIPPEN

Scottie Pippen played most of his career in the shadow of the great Michael Jordan. Together they led the Chicago Bulls to six NBA championships. Jordan was the NBA Finals MVP all six times. Pippen was more than a capable sidekick, though. And he more than proved that in Jordan's absence.

The Bulls won their first three titles in 1991, 1992, and 1993. Then Jordan unexpectedly retired. Jordan had been the biggest star in the game. But Pippen stepped out of his shadow with a season to remember.

With Jordan gone, opponents lined their best defenders against Pippen. Yet the Bulls' forward still averaged a career-high 22.0 points per game.

Chicago Bulls forward Scottie Pippen controls the ball during a 1992 game against the Atlanta Hawks.

Pippen also grabbed 8.7 rebounds per game, which was another career high. Add in 2.9 steals and 5.6 assists per contest, and it was clear that Pippen was a superstar in his own right. The only mark against Pippen's career was that he never won an NBA title without Jordan. But Pippen was a key player on the Bulls' six championship teams. They also won the title in 1996, 1997, and 1998.

Pippen was the perfect fit for his role with the Bulls. He handled the ball well enough to play point guard when needed. He could score like a small forward to complement Jordan's explosive offensive game. He was strong enough to battle power forwards for rebounds. And he was able to defend any of those positions.

Pippen was a proven winner. His teams reached the playoffs in each of his 16 full NBA seasons. He also won two Olympic gold medals, in 1992 and 1996.

2

The number of times Scottie Pippen won an Olympic gold medal and an NBA title in the same year (1992, 1996). No player had matched that going into the 2016 Olympics.

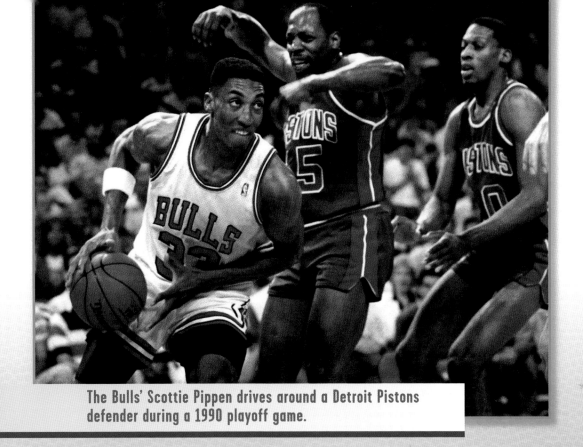

The Bulls' Scottie Pippen drives around a Detroit Pistons defender during a 1990 playoff game.

SCOTTIE PIPPEN

Hometown: Hamburg, Arkansas

College: University of Central Arkansas

Height, Weight: 6 feet 8, 210 pounds

Birth Date: September 25 ,1965

Teams: Chicago Bulls (1987–98, 2003–04)
Houston Rockets (1999)
Portland Trail Blazers (1999–2003)

All-Star Games: 7 (1990, 1992–97)

First-Team All-NBA: 1993–94, 1994–95, 1995–96

All-Defensive Team: 1991–92, 1992–93, 1993–94, 1994–95, 1995–96, 1996–97, 1997–98, 1998–99

KEVIN GARNETT

Kevin Garnett began his career with the Minnesota Timberwolves. He carried that team on his back for 12 seasons. Yet only once did the team advance beyond the playoffs' first round. By 2007, Minnesota needed to rebuild. So the team traded its star to the Boston Celtics. At age 31, Garnett finally felt like he had a chance to win his first NBA title. And he was right.

The Celtics had a talented, veteran team. They needed one more piece to complete the puzzle. Garnett was that piece. He became the first Celtics player to win the NBA Defensive Player of the Year Award. He then helped Boston reach the NBA Finals. It was the storied team's first NBA Finals appearance in 21 years. There, they met the archrival Los Angeles Lakers.

Minnesota Timberwolves forward Kevin Garnett rises into the air for a shot against the Indiana Pacers in 1997.

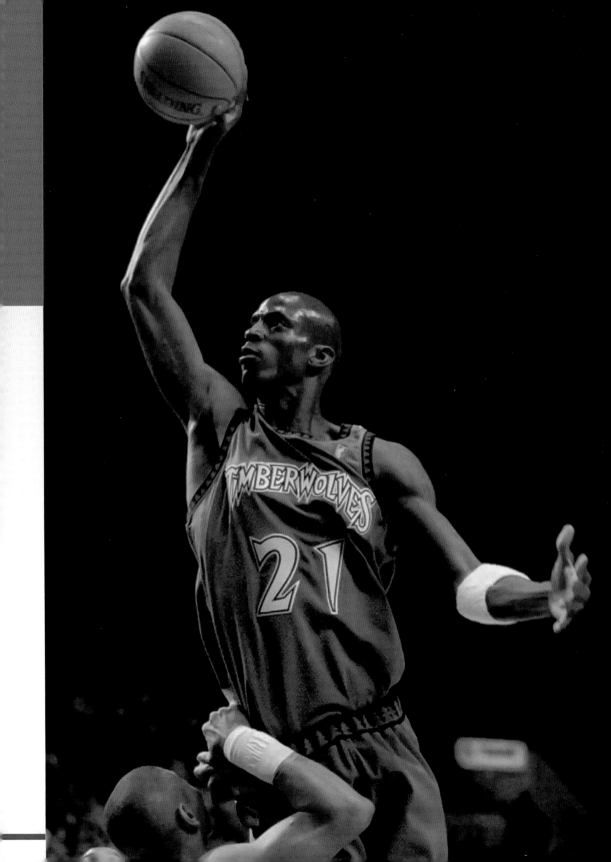

It was no contest. The Celtics won the championship in six games. They blew out the Lakers by 39 points in the deciding game. The Boston crowd roared. The players spilled onto the floor to celebrate. A TV reporter met Garnett during the celebration. Overcome by emotion, Garnett could barely gather himself to answer a question. Finally, he leaned back, looked to the sky, and screamed, "Anything is possible!"

Garnett had gone straight into the NBA out of high school. That was a controversial decision at the time. But he was an instant success. His height made him tough for forwards to defend. And centers could not handle his quickness. Garnett led the NBA in rebounding four times through 2013. However, he will likely be remembered most for the passion he displayed every time he stepped onto the court.

6

The number of consecutive seasons in which Kevin Garnett averaged at least 20 points, 10 rebounds, and five assists per game. That was still an NBA record through 2013.

The Boston Celtics' Kevin Garnett moves past an Atlanta Hawks defender during a 2008 game.

KEVIN GARNETT

Hometown: Mauldin, South Carolina

High School: Farragut Career Academy, Chicago, Illinois

Height, Weight: 6 feet 11, 220 pounds

Birth Date: May 19, 1976

Teams: Minnesota Timberwolves (1995–2007)
  Boston Celtics (2007–13)
  Brooklyn Nets (2013–)

All-Star Games: 15 (1997–98, 2000–11, 2013)

MVP Award: 2003–04

First-Team All-NBA: 1999–2000, 2002–03, 2003–04, 2007–08

All-Defensive Team: 1999–2000, 2000–01, 2001–02, 2002–03, 2003–04, 2004–05, 2007–08, 2008–09, 2010–11

53

TIM DUNCAN

If it were not for a natural disaster, Tim Duncan might never have reached the NBA. Duncan grew up in the US Virgin Islands. Swimming was his first true love. He was good at it, too. In fact, he was the top US swimmer in his age group in the 400-meter freestyle event.

But everything changed for Duncan in 1989. A massive hurricane hit the Virgin Islands. His hometown of St. Croix was hit hard. An estimated 90 percent of the buildings were damaged or destroyed. One of those buildings was the town's only Olympic-sized swimming pool. The 13-year-old Duncan needed to find a new sport.

He turned to basketball. Duncan grew 9 inches (23 cm) in high school. That helped him catch the attention of college coaches. Duncan decided to play for Wake Forest University.

San Antonio Spurs forward Tim Duncan drives for a dunk during a 2006 game against the Minnesota Timberwolves.

He became an All-American during his time at the North Carolina school. Then the San Antonio Spurs picked him first overall in the 1997 NBA Draft.

The Spurs already were a good team. However, a bit of luck helped them land Duncan. Star center David Robinson had gotten injured the year before. He missed all but six games. Without him, the Spurs won only 20 games. Then they won the draft lottery to get the first overall pick.

Duncan is nicknamed "The Big Fundamental." That is because everything he does is technically sound. He is an excellent rebounder. He is impossible to defend in the low post. Plus, he is an excellent defender and shot blocker. Through 2013, Duncan had led the Spurs to four NBA titles. He had also averaged more than 20 points and 11 rebounds per game in his career.

3

The number of NBA Finals MVP Awards Tim Duncan won in his first three tries. He became only the second player after Michael Jordan to accomplish that feat.

The Spurs' Tim Duncan shoots over a New Orleans Hornets defender during a 2007 game.

TIM DUNCAN

Hometown: St. Croix, US Virgin Islands

College: Wake Forest University

Height, Weight: 6 feet 11, 248 pounds

Birth Date: April 25, 1976

Team: San Antonio Spurs (1997–)

All-Star Games: 14 (1998, 2000–11, 2013)

MVP Awards: 2001–02, 2002–03

First-Team All-NBA: 1997–98, 1998–99, 1999–2000, 2000–01, 2001–02, 2002–03, 2003–04, 2004–05, 2006–07, 2012–13

All-Defensive Team: 1998–99, 1999–2000, 2000–01, 2001–02, 2002–03, 2004–05, 2006–07, 2007–08

LeBRON JAMES

LeBron James already was regarded as the best player in the NBA. A crushing loss in 2011 helped make him even better.

Most people favored James's Miami Heat to win the NBA title that year. But James struggled against the Dallas Mavericks in the NBA Finals. The Mavericks' tight defense held James to just 17.8 points per game. In the regular season, he had averaged 26.7 points. Dallas ended up winning the title in six games, and James took the defeat personally.

James had always had amazing talent. And he had always been able to rely on that talent to outplay opponents. That was not the case in the 2011 Finals, though. He realized he would have to work harder to improve his skills. In particular, he knew his low-post game had to get better. So James called on Hall of Fame center Hakeem Olajuwon for help.

LeBron James of the Miami Heat looks to pass during the 2013 NBA Finals against the San Antonio Spurs.

Olajuwon helped James learn how to take advantage of his size and quickness. That helped James become more effective closer to the basket.

When he came back the next season, James was a new man. He dominated games down low. That helped him set up his teammates for open shots outside. By the end of the year, James had not only won his third NBA MVP Award. He had also won his first NBA championship.

James was the first pick of the 2003 NBA Draft. His hometown Cleveland Cavaliers had taken him straight out of high school. James put up amazing numbers in seven years with the Cavaliers. However, the team only reached the NBA Finals once during that span. So in 2010, James signed with Miami. In 2013, he led the Heat to its third straight Finals appearance and its second consecutive NBA title.

25

The number of points LeBron James scored in his first NBA game. That was the most for a player making his debut straight out of high school.

The Heat's LeBron James dunks the ball during a 2013 NBA playoff game against the Indiana Pacers.

LeBRON JAMES

Hometown: Akron, Ohio

High School: Saint Vincent-Saint Mary, Akron, Ohio

Height, Weight: 6 feet 8, 240 pounds

Birth Date: December 30, 1984

Teams: Cleveland Cavaliers (2003–10)
Miami Heat (2010–)

All-Star Games: 10 (2005–14)

MVP Awards: 2008–09, 2009–10, 2011–12, 2012–13

First-Team All-NBA: 2005–06, 2007–08, 2008–09, 2009–10,
2010–11, 2011–12, 2012–13

All-Defensive Team: 2008–09, 2009–10, 2010–11, 2011–12,
2012–13

HONORABLE MENTIONS

Kevin Durant – One of the NBA's most lethal scorers, Durant won three scoring titles in a row from 2009–10 to 2011–12 and led the Oklahoma City Thunder to the 2012 NBA Finals.

Alex English – A fixture with the Denver Nuggets in the 1980s, English played in eight All-Star Games and is ranked tenth on the all-time career field goals list.

Jerry Lucas – Lucas was a star from the mid-1960s to the mid-1970s with the Cincinnati Royals, the San Francisco Warriors, and the New York Knicks. A two-time First-Team All-NBA selection, Lucas ranked fourth all-time in career rebounds per game through 2013.

Chris Mullin – A deadly shooter and slick passer, Mullin starred for the Golden State Warriors and the Indiana Pacers from 1985 to 2001.

Dirk Nowitzki – A native of Germany, Nowitzki helped spread the popularity of the NBA in Europe, while winning one NBA title and one league MVP Award for the Dallas Mavericks in the 2000s. Nowitzki is a rare power forward who can sink three-pointers.

Dennis Rodman – One of the NBA's greatest rebounders and defenders, Rodman won NBA titles with the Detroit Pistons in 1989 and 1990 and three more with the Chicago Bulls in the late 1990s.

Dolph Schayes – Schayes was one of the NBA's pioneers with the Syracuse Nationals in the 1950s, averaging double figures in scoring and rebounding for 11 straight years.

Dominique Wilkins – Wilkins was the high-flying star of the Atlanta Hawks who wowed NBA fans during the 1980s with his amazing dunks.

James Worthy – Worthy was a key player in the Los Angeles Lakers' 1980s dynasty, winning three NBA titles and one NBA Finals MVP Award.

GLOSSARY

assist
A pass that leads directly to a basket.

blocked shot
A play in which a shooter's field goal attempt is knocked down by a defender before it can reach the rim.

defense
The act of trying to stop your opponent from scoring a basket.

low post
The area on the court near the basket, where centers and power forwards often set up during action.

rebound
A recovery of a missed shot.

rookie
A first-year player in the NBA.

sixth man
A name given to the first player off the bench on a basketball team.

steal
A statistic awarded to a player who takes the ball away from an opponent or intercepts a pass intended for an opponent.

veteran
A player with a lot of experience.

FOR MORE INFORMATION

Further Readings

Silverman, Drew. *Basketball*. Minneapolis, MN: Abdo Publishing Co., 2012.

Silverman, Drew. *The NBA Finals*. Minneapolis, MN: Abdo Publishing Co., 2013.

Websites

To learn more about NBA's Best Ever, visit **booklinks.abdopublishing.com**. These links are routinely monitored and updated to provide the most current information available.

INDEX

ABOUT THE AUTHOR

Patrick Donnelly is a veteran sportswriter who has covered the NBA, NFL, MLB, NHL, NASCAR, PGA, and college and prep sports for the Associated Press, MLB.com, and other websites and publications throughout the United States. He lives in Minneapolis, Minnesota, with his wife and two daughters.